Poetry about Cakes and Desserts

Titles also, by Dave Charles

The Consequences of War – Contemporary Poetry, and Haiku about War, Conflict, and PTSD.

The Scottish Wilderness – Poetry, and Haiku about Scotland, Nature, Places, Lochs, and Glens.

Ancient Alien Theorists Compendium of Poetry and Short Stories – The Ancient Alien Agenda, Reports of Sightings, Ancient Locations on Earth, and Out-of-Place Artefacts Found on Our Planet.

Finding Inner Peace - PTSD Survivors Guide, Poetry, and Helpful Information to Find Inner Peace, and to Aid Recovery.

Between Heaven and Earth – A Guide to Majestic Scottish Castles, Best Castle Gardens, Monuments, Tourist Attractions, Battle Sites, Golf Courses, Beaches, and Whisky Distilleries.

Treasure Hunting the Ultimate Guide – Metal Detecting, Gold Panning, Magnet Fishing, River Hunting, Fossil, and Gem Hunting, Bottle Digging, Beachcombing, and Shipwreck Diving.

Into The Wild – An Anthology of Wildlife Poetry from the Animal Kingdom.

Gulf War Syndrome – A Guide to this Debilitating Illness, from Service in the First Gulf War.

Courage Under Fire – The Story of My British Army Career, and the Historical Aspects Behind Military Events During This Time.

How To Regulate Your Emotions – Self-Help Regulating Your Emotions, Gaining Confidence and Self-Esteem.

Gods and Goddesses – Mythology or Ancient Astronaut's Visiting Earth?

The Jilted Generation – Poetry and Haiku about Nature, Places, Emotions, Love, and Life Stories.

150 Historical Geniuses – Stories of the world's most historical geniuses, people with high IQs that change the world for all of us.

Love Poems – Poetry about Love, Loss, Romance, Desires, Hopes and Dreams.

Ancient Egyptian New Kingdom – The 18th, 19th and 20th Dynasties and Pharaohs Listed in Order of their Reigns.

Poetry about
Cakes and Desserts

Dave Charles

Text and Cover Images Copyright © Dave Charles

All rights reserved.

No part of this book may be reproduced in any form or by any electronic or mechanical means including information storage and retrieval systems, without permission in writing from the author. The only exception is by a reviewer, who may quote short excerpts in a review.

About the Author

I was born in Oxford, England and moved to Manchester when I was six. I joined the army at sixteen.

I served in the British Army for many years. I am a veteran of the late Cold War era, having served in the former West Germany between 1984 and 1989.

I later served in Saudi Arabia and Iraq during the first Persian Gulf War in 1991 as part of 'Operation Granby' or as the U.S. termed 'Desert Storm.' I then served with the United Nations, undertaking peacekeeping tours in Cyprus and Bosnia during the 1990s. I also served in many other countries.

After leaving the armed forces, I was diagnosed with complex combat PTSD and numerous other medical conditions and mental health issues.

This took many years and eventual therapy to recover from; although I will always be in recovery from PTSD, it is now under control and manageable. Writing and Poetry have been an integral part of my recovery process.

Chocolate Chip Cookies

In the kitchen, a dance of dough and delight,
Sugar and butter, a harmonious sight.
Golden brown edges, a sweet, warm embrace,
Chocolate chips melting, a smile on each face.

A hint of vanilla, a dash of pure love,
Each bite a treasure, like stars up above.
Soft and chewy, or crispy and thin,
Chocolate chip cookies, a joy to begin.

From childhood memories to moments anew,
They comfort and cheer with each bite we chew.
A timeless treat, perfect in every way,
Chocolate chip cookies, brightening our day.

Fruit Scones

In a quaint English garden, where the roses bloom bright,
Lies a table set for tea, in the soft morning light.
A porcelain teapot, with steam gently rising,
Beside it, a platter that's simply enticing.

Golden scones, fresh and warm from the oven's embrace,
Their buttery scent fills the air, a tender grace.
Split open with care, a delicate scene,
Spread with rich jam, and a dollop of cream.

Oh, the dance of flavours, so sweet and divine,
The tartness of berries, with cream so fine.
Each bite is a journey, a comforting dream,
In the heart of the garden, with scones, jam, and cream.

So gather your loved ones, let the moments be shared,
For in these simple pleasures, true joy is declared.
With laughter and stories, beneath skies so serene,
Life's sweetest indulgence: jam and cream scones, a timeless cuisine.

Doughnuts

In a cozy shop, at break of day,
Doughnuts lie in sweet array.
Golden rings and twists delight,
Sprinkled, glazed, a sugary sight.

Yeast and flour, a tender blend,
In the fryer, they descend.
Rising, browning, puffy dreams,
Dusted lightly, chocolate streams.

Morning's joy, a baker's pride,
Warmth and comfort deep inside.
Round confections, circles spun,
With each bite, a day begun.

Apple Pie

Crimson skin with a glossy sheen,
In the heart of autumn, an apple's dream.

Peel and slice with tender care,
Each piece a promise, a love affair,
With sugar and spice, a dash of delight,
Cinnamon whispers in the soft twilight.

In the oven's embrace, it starts to bloom,
Golden crust, dispelling gloom,
A slice of heaven, in a dish, lies,
A timeless joy, an apple pie.

Rhubarb Crumble

In gardens where sunlight dances and gleams,
Rhubarb grows in verdant dreams,
Stalks so tender, leaves so wide,
Nature's sweetness, a hidden pride.

Picked with care, in hands so light,
A harvest brought to kitchen's sight,
Chopped and sugared, ruby red,
A rustic dish soon to be fed.

Crumble topping, golden, fine,
Oats and butter, sweet design,
Into the oven, warmth and glow,
Baking memories, love bestows.

As the scent fills every room,
Hearts are lifted, banishing gloom,
A rhubarb crumble, simple and true,
A taste of comfort, through and through.

Bread and Butter Pudding

Bread and butter, sweet and bright,
Transforms the day and warms the night.

Golden slices, layered with care,
Butter melts, a luscious affair,

Custard poured, a silky stream,
A cozy, comforting dream.

Raisins, plump, and cinnamon's kiss,
Simple pleasures, pure bliss,

From oven's heart, a hug in disguise,
Bread and butter pudding, love's reprise.

Twinkies

In the land of golden treats, a legend does reside,
A pillowy delight, where joy and sweetness hide.
Twinkies, oh Twinkies, with your spongy embrace,
A bite of nostalgia, a moment to chase.

Wrapped in a golden glow, a treasure to unfold,
Inside, a creamy heart, a story to be told.
Soft as a whisper, light as a summer's breeze,
You bring back childhood smiles with effortless ease.

From lunchbox surprises to midnight's secret crave,
Twinkies, your charm, our hearts you do enslave.
In a world of fleeting fads, your magic stays true,
A timeless confection, forever adored by me and you.

Chocolate Éclair

In the heart of the bakery, where sweet dreams reside,
Lies a treasure of cocoa, with a golden outside.
A delicate pastry, light as the air,
Behold the enchantment of the Chocolate Eclair.

With a touch of finesse, and a masterful hand,
Pastry cream fills it, as if by command.
A rich velvet centre, so luscious and fair,
Encased in the magic of the Chocolate Eclair.

Topped with a glaze, dark chocolate divine,
Each bite is a journey, transcending through time.
A symphony of flavours, beyond all compare,
Such is the wonder of the Chocolate Eclair.

Vanilla Slice

In a bakery's warm embrace, under golden morning light,
Lies a treasure, sweet and pure, a true confectionery delight.
Layers crisp, with tender care, baked to a buttery sheen,
Vanilla slice, enchantment fair, a royal dessert cuisine.

Custard rich and velvet smooth, nestled in between,
A cream-filled dream, a silken touch, like whispers so serene.
Sweet as a summer's day, with flavour bold yet mild,
Each bite a dance, a symphony, that leaves your heart beguiled.

Dust of sugar, gentle snow, upon the final crust,
A pastry kiss, a tender hug, a taste you learn to trust.
Oh, vanilla slice, you captivate, in every luscious bite,
A timeless treat, a love affair, with every sweet delight.

Strawberry Tart

Tender berries, kissed by the sun,
Whisper secrets of summer fun.

Their fragrance dances, a gentle breeze,
A promise of joy, an ease to please.

Creamy whispers, atop they lie,
A cloud of delight, a sugary sky.

In every bite, a story's told,
Of love and laughter, pure and bold.

So here's to the tart, with strawberry grace,
A dessert that brings smiles to every face.

May every slice, with bliss impart,
The magic of a strawberry tart.

Genoa Cake

In a kitchen warm with festive cheer,
A Genoa cake begins to appear.
With fruits and nuts, a rich delight,
It bakes and fills the home with light.

Candied peels and cherries red,
In a batter, richly spread.
Almonds, walnuts, each a gem,
Folded gently, added then.

Golden brown, it cools with grace,
A masterpiece that time can't erase.
Shared with love and laughter free,
A slice of joy for you and me.

Battenberg

In a world of sweet delight, behold the sight,
A cake so charming, dressed in pink and white,
Battenberg, a marvel, a checkerboard of glee,
Wrapped in marzipan, a treat for you and me.

Squares so perfect, nestled side by side,
Almond essence whispers, flavours that collide,
A pattern of joy in every slice we take,
History and sweetness in a Battenberg cake.

With every bite, memories unfold,
Of tea-time tales in days of old,
A cake that bridges past and present streams,
Battenberg, a confection of dreams.

Madeleines

In a quaint café, where time does softly tread,
A plate of madeleines, their fragrance spread,

With golden curves and scalloped grace,
They whisper secrets of a sweeter place.

Buttery whispers, tender bites suffice,
Each crumb a memory, a moment's spice,

Transported back to days of yore,
Where childhood dreams and laughter soar.

Dundee Cake

In Scotland's heart, where tales are spun,
Lies Dundee cake, kissed by the sun.
With almonds strewn atop so neat,
A Scottish treat, both dense and sweet.

The orange peel, so candied bright,
Gives zest and tang, a pure delight.
Raisins, sultanas, currants blend,
In each warm bite, traditions mend.

From ancient kitchens, whispers bake,
The spirit of Dundee cake.
A slice of heritage, rich and grand,
A timeless joy in every hand.

Tunis Cake

In a bakery's warm embrace,
Lies a treat with timeless grace,
A Tunis Cake, rich and sweet,
A festive delight, a joyous feat.

Golden sponge, so soft and light,
Baked to perfection, pure delight,
A crown of marzipan so fine,
Decorates this cake divine.

Candied fruits, a vibrant hue,
Adorn the top, a colourful view,
With every bite, a journey takes,
Through memories that Tunis Cake makes.

A slice of warmth, a taste of cheer,
Brings loved ones close, year after year,
In every crumb, in every bite,
The spirit of joy, the essence of light.

Rum Baba

In a land where sweetness reigns supreme,
There lives a treat that haunts the dream,
A Rum Baba, with its golden gleam,
A pastry soaked in syrup's gleam.

Born from dough so light and airy,
With a heart that sings of rum and berry,
It dances on the tongue so merry,
A symphony both bold and fairy.

Drizzled with a glaze divine,
Each bite a sip of nectar's wine,
In every crumb, a secret sign,
Of indulgence pure, a taste refined.

Oh, Rum Baba, delightful sprite,
You bring to life the darkest night,
A moment's bliss, a pure delight,
In every bite, the world's made right.

Profiteroles

In the heart of a patisserie, dreams unfold,
Where golden choux puffs, warm and bold,
Nestle close, a tale of delight they tell,
Profiteroles, where sweet desires dwell.

Crisp exteriors, a whisper of grace,
Encasing treasures, a soft embrace,
Velvet cream within, a secret shared,
Each bite, a moment tenderly cared.

Cloaked in chocolate, a luscious sheen,
A masterpiece, a confectioner's dream,
Profiteroles, a symphony of taste,
Moments of joy, never to waste.

Cream Horns

In the bakery's warm embrace, they lie,
Golden crescents that catch the eye.
Spirals of pastry, so light and sweet,
A promise of delight in every bite we meet.

Flaky and tender, they curl with grace,
Sugar-dusted dreams in a delicate case.
Inside, a treasure of creamy delight,
A whisper of heaven in the soft morning light.

Oh, cream horns, you bring such cheer,
A bite of joy, pure and clear.
In every layer, a story unfolds,
Of buttery bliss and secrets untold.

Danish Pastries

In a cozy Danish bakery, warm and bright,
Where the morning sun kisses the dough just right,
Lies a pastry, golden with a sugary glaze,
A symphony of flavours, a culinary praise.

Layers of flakiness, delicate and light,
With buttery whispers that melt at first bite,
Almonds and custard embrace in sweet dance,
A taste of enchantment, a momentous romance.

Oh, Danish Pastry, you bring such delight,
With each tender morsel, the world feels right,
A slice of joy in every crumb and flake,
A timeless treasure in each cake we partake.

Pain au Chocolat

Golden layers, crisp and light,
Morning's promise, pure delight.
A delicate dance of dough and butter,
Whispers of Parisian streets in each flutter.

Rich and dark, the heart concealed,
Chocolate treasures, once revealed.
Melted dreams in a flaky embrace,
A taste of elegance, a moment of grace.

In every bite, a story told,
Of artisan hands and secrets old.
Pain au Chocolat, a symphony sweet,
A timeless treat for hearts to meet.

Yum Tum

In a world of flavours, a delight so true,
Yum Yum whispers, "I am here for you."
A dance of taste upon the tongue,
A melody of joy forever sung.

Sweet and savoury, a blissful embrace,
Each bite a journey, a heavenly trace.
From rich chocolate to golden crust,
In Yum Yum's realm, we place our trust.

Moments of pleasure, wrapped in delight,
Yum Yum brings magic, morning to night.
A symphony of flavours, a feast for the soul,
In every morsel, we find ourselves whole.

Chocolate Brownies

With the air filled with sweet delight,
Lies a treasure dark as night,
A square of joy, a simple treat,
Chocolate brownies, oh, so sweet.

Cocoa whispers, sugar sings,
Butter dreams of wondrous things,
Flour and eggs blend in a dance,
Creating magic in a trance.

Baked to perfection, warm and true,
With a crust that calls to you,
Inside, a heart so soft and pure,
A bite of bliss, forever sure.

Each morsel, rich, a love profound,
A taste where heaven can be found,
Chocolate brownies, pure delight,
In every bite, both day and night.

Cup Cakes

In a bakery's warm and fragrant light,
Cupcakes stand, a colourful delight.
Frosting swirls in peaks so high,
Underneath a sugar sky.

Vanilla whispers, chocolate dreams,
Red velvet's whispers, berry streams.
Sprinkles dance like stars above,
Each bite a moment filled with love.

From birthdays bright to simple days,
Cupcakes sweeten life's small ways.
A tiny cake, a joy to share,
A little bliss beyond compare.

Blueberry Muffins

Bursting berries, blue and bright,
Hidden gems in golden light,
Soft and tender, baked with care,
A taste of love beyond compare.

With each bite, a smile grows,
A comfort that the heart well knows,
Blueberry muffins, fresh and true,
A morning gift, from me to you.

As the day begins with such delight,
A promise of a day that's bright,
The warmth of home, the love it shows,
In every crumb, the joy that flows.

The kitchen's hum, the morning song,
Where cherished moments all belong,
A ritual of love and light,
To start the day with pure delight.

So take this gift, enjoy it well,
In every bite, a story to tell,
Blueberry muffins, warm and sweet,
A simple joy, a cozy treat.

Snowball

In a winter's dream, a treat divine,
A snowball cake with a frosted shine,
Soft and round, like a snowflake's kiss,
A confectionary bliss, pure and fine.

Coconut whispers on a bed of white,
Sponge cake nestled, a sweet delight,
Creamy middle, a hidden surprise,
With every bite, a taste that flies.

Winter's magic in every slice,
A snowy wonder, a pure delight,
Snowball cake, a festive cheer,
Bringing warmth and joy, year after year.

Red Velvet Cake

In a world of desserts, one stands supreme,
A slice of heaven, a baker's dream.
Red Velvet Cake, with layers so fine,
A crimson delight, a taste so divine.

Cream cheese frosting, a crown of white,
Soft and smooth, a pure delight.
Buttermilk whispers, cocoa's embrace,
A dance of flavours, a sweet, tender grace.

Each bite a journey, rich and grand,
A symphony of taste, a lover's command.
Red Velvet Cake, a timeless art,
Forever cherished, a piece of my heart.

Banana Bread

From speckled fruit, once past its prime,
Comes magic in moments, a taste so sublime.
Mashed with care, mixed with flair,
Love in each slice, beyond compare.

In morning light or evening's hush,
Its aroma lingers, a gentle brush.
A testament to patience, to the love we spread,
In every loaf of banana bread.

Warm from the oven, it's a family affair,
A slice for each, memories to share.
With each tender bite, a story unfolds,
Of kitchens past and hearts of gold.

So when life's moments start to fray,
Take a breath, and bake away.
For in the mix of flour and ripe delight,
You'll find a piece of home each night.

A gentle reminder in our fast-paced age,
That joy can be simple, as wisdom sage.
In every crumb, a story's told,
Of love, tradition, and warmth to hold.

Rock Cake

In a quaint kitchen, where memories bake,
Sits a humble treat, the beloved rock cake.
With butter and sugar, flour so fine,
A touch of spice, a zest of time.

Golden brown crust, rugged and sweet,
A history rich in every bite we meet.
Raisins and currants, gems in the dough,
A simple delight, from long ago.

No icing or frills, just warmth you can hold,
A rock cake's story, timelessly told.
With each crumbly mouthful, a moment to share,
A taste of tradition, beyond compare.

Sponge Cream Cake

In a kitchen warm with morning light,
A baker toils with gentle might,
She smooths the batter, rich and sweet,
For cream sponge cake, a timeless treat.

Golden layers rise with care,
A fragrant promise fills the air,
Soft as clouds, they cool and rest,
Awaiting love's sweetest test.

Whipped cream swirls in peaks so high,
Like snowy drifts against the sky,
Sandwiched 'tween each tender slice,
A dance of textures, pure delight.

A sprinkle of sugar, a final grace,
Transforms the cake to a magic place,
With every bite, a dream retold,
A symphony of flavours, pure and bold.

So let us gather, friends and kin,
Around this cake, let joy begin,
For in each crumb, a story's spun,
Of love, and life, and days in sun.

Mince Pies

In the heart of winter, as chill winds blow,
A warming scent begins to flow.
From kitchens bright with festive cheer,
The fruit mince pies, so dear, appear.

Golden crusts with a gentle flake,
Encasing treasures bakers make.
A symphony of fruits and spice,
Each bite a portal to paradise.

Cinnamon whispers a tale of old,
While nutmeg and cloves in warmth enfold.
Raisins and currants, candied peels,
Together in harmony, a joy that heals.

These humble pies, a festive rite,
Gleam like stars on a frosty night.
Shared with loved ones, hearts draw near,
In every slice, the spirit of the year.

Coconut Cake

In a tropical breeze where the palm trees sway,
Lies a treasure of sweetness, in layers it lay.
Golden and tender, with a sprinkle of white,
A coconut cake, a pure delight.

Fluffy as clouds on a clear summer's day,
Its frosting is silk, smooth in every way.
With each bite a journey, to islands afar,
Where the scent of the ocean, and coconut are.

Oh, coconut cake, with your charm so divine,
In you, the essence of paradise we find.
A symphony of flavours, a dance on the tongue,
A slice of sheer bliss when the day is done.

Black Forest Gateau

In the heart of a forest, dark and deep,
Lies a gateau that makes taste buds weep.
Layers of chocolate, as rich as night,
With cherries that add a tangy delight.

Whipped cream clouds, so pure and white,
Nestle between, a heavenly sight.
Each bite whispers secrets of the trees,
A dance of flavours that aims to please.

Oh, Black Forest Gateau, a treat so fine,
A slice of magic, truly divine.
With every mouthful, a journey to take,
Through the enchanted forest, wide awake.

Manchester Tart

In Manchester's heart, a tart so sweet,
A culinary gem, a local treat.
With golden crust, so tender, light,
It brings pure joy with every bite.

A layer rich of custard pure,
Its creamy touch, a taste so sure.
Beneath, the jam, a ruby gleam,
A burst of fruit, a sugar dream.

Crowned with coconut, snowy white,
A sprinkle soft, a pure delight.
In every slice, a piece of art,
The beloved, famed Manchester Tart.

Banoffee Pie

In a crust so crisp and golden bright,
Banoffee Pie, a sheer delight.
With layers rich and flavours bold,
A sweet indulgence to behold.

Bananas soft, in caramel's embrace,
Create a symphony of taste.
A whisper of cream, so light and airy,
Crowning it all, so sweet and merry.

Each bite a blend of dreams divine,
A dance of textures, so sublime.
In Banoffee's spell, we gladly lie,
A slice of heaven, in a pie.

Piquant Pie

In the kitchen, scents arise,
A piquant pie, a sweet surprise.
Crust of golden, flaky dreams,
Fills the air with tempting themes.

Spices dance in fragrant swirls,
Nutmeg, cinnamon, in twirls.
Apples, peaches, berries blend,
A symphony that has no end.

Bite by bite, the flavours sing,
On taste buds, joy they bring.
Piquant pie, a heart's delight,
A masterpiece in every bite.

Knickerbocker Glory

In a glass so tall and grand,
A marvel from a dessert land,
Knickerbocker Glory stands so proud,
A treat that gathers quite a crowd.

Layers bright with colours bold,
A story of flavours yet untold,
First, the fruits, a juicy start,
A burst of joy to warm the heart.

Ice cream scoops like snowy peaks,
Melting slowly, soft and sleek,
Whipped cream clouds sit on top,
A cascade sweet, no need to stop.

Sprinkles rain, a festive cheer,
A spoonful brings the magic near,
Cherry crowned, a ruby gleam,
A knickerbocker glory, the ultimate dream.

New York Cheesecake

In the heart of a city that never sleeps,
Lies a treasure, a secret it keeps.
A slice of heaven, rich and divine,
New York cheesecake, simply sublime.

Golden crust with a buttery embrace,
Silky smooth filling, a delicate grace.
Each bite a journey, a creamy delight,
A symphony of flavours in the moonlight.

Beneath the skyline, where dreams take flight,
New York cheesecake, a beacon of light.
From the bustling streets to quiet nooks,
It's a taste of the city in every look.

Upside Down Cake

In a world where sweet confections reign,
There lies a cake, a twist so plain.
Upside down, a curious sight,
A dance of flavours, pure delight.

Golden pineapples crown its face,
In caramel's sweet, sticky embrace.
Cherries rest in ruby hue,
A picture painted, bright and true.

Baked with love and turned around,
A masterpiece, both soft and sound.
Upside down, yet standing tall,
A cake that brings joy to all.

Strawberry Mousse

In a bowl of satin dreams, so light,
A dance of strawberries, pure delight,
Whipped to clouds, with sugar kissed,
A summer's essence cannot be missed.

Creamy whispers, a blush so fair,
Echoes of gardens, fragrant air,
Each spoonful tells a tale anew,
Of morning dew and skies of blue.

Oh, strawberry mousse, sweet and bright,
A symphony of pink, a soft twilight,
In every bite, a moment stays,
Of sunlit fields and golden days.

Ice Cream

In the summer's golden, sunlit gleam,
I find solace in my love of ice-cream.
A delight that dances on my tongue,
Sweet symphony, forever young.

Vanilla whispers, soft and pure,
A classic love, that's always sure.
Chocolate rivers, rich and deep,
A velvety dream, in which I sleep.

Strawberry fields, a berry's bliss,
Each spoonful like a gentle kiss.
Minty fresh, with chocolate chips,
A cooling breeze, at my lips.

Rainbow swirls in vibrant hues,
A prism of flavours, joyous news.
From waffle cones to sundae bowls,
This creamy love consumes my soul.

In every scoop, a story told,
Of comfort sweet and joy so bold.
Oh, icy treat, my heart's delight,
You make my world so pure and bright.

Meringue Nests

In kitchens warm with sugared air,
Where hands so deftly craft with care,
A dance of whisk and egg whites bright,
Transforms the dusk to pure delight.

Soft peaks arise like clouds so fair,
To float on breeze with tender flair,
A swirl of sweetness, crisp and light,
A meringue nest in the moon's soft light.

Upon this nest, a treasure rare,
Fruit jewels gleam, a vibrant pair,
Each bite a symphony, sheer delight,
A heavenly treat, both day and night.

Souffle Pudding

Whisked with care, each fold a grace,
Eggs and sugar in a gentle embrace.

A cloud of sweetness, baked to rise,
Golden peaks that mesmerise.

With every spoonful, a tender bite,
Melts on the tongue, a pure delight.

Soufflé pudding, a fleeting pleasure,
A moment savoured, eternal treasure.

Soufflé pudding, light as air,
A culinary dream, beyond compare.

A masterpiece on the plate, divine and rare,
Soufflé pudding, a joy to share.

Jelly and Ice-Cream

In a bowl so bright, a childhood dream,
Lies a dance of jelly and ice-cream.
Colours swirl in a sweet embrace,
A symphony of joy in every taste.

The jelly, wobbly, a prism of delight,
Reflects the sun in a soft, gentle light.
Raspberry red or lime green glow,
A playful jig, a whimsical show.

Ice-cream scoops, so creamy and cold,
Vanilla, chocolate, or strawberry bold.
Melting slowly, they blend with the jell,
Creating magic, a story to tell.

Together they sit, a nostalgic treat,
Reminding us of summers, tender and sweet.
In each bite, a memory gleams,
The simple joy of jelly and ice-cream.

Viennetta

In the realm of desserts, a marvel so grand,
Viennetta pudding, a delight so well-planned.
Layers of bliss, where chocolate meets cream,
A culinary wonder, a sweet lover's dream.

Velvet ripples of richness cascade,
Each bite a moment, where worries fade.
From the first gentle spoonful to the last,
A timeless indulgence, both present and past.

Oh, Viennetta, with elegance you stand,
A symphony of flavours, pure and unplanned.
In your icy embrace, joy we find,
A testament to sweetness, forever enshrined.

Arctic Roll

In the frosty realms where the chill winds blow,
A sweet delight, the Arctic Roll does glow.
A swirl of sponge, with ice cream pure and white,
Encased in joy, a frozen, creamy bite.

With every slice, a memory unfolds,
Of winter nights and tales the hearth once told.
The cake, a blanket wrapped around the ice,
A dance of textures, oh so very nice.

From childhood dreams to festive tables set,
The Arctic Roll, we never will forget.
A timeless treat in snow-kissed lands of old,
A story sweet, forever to be told.

Swiss Roll

In a baker's dream, where sweetness meets,
A Swiss roll waits in swirling sheets.
With tender sponge and creamy core,
It's a delight we all adore.

Twirling like a dancer's spin,
Vanilla or with chocolate pinned,
Each bite a journey, rich and light,
A symphony of pure delight.

Wrapped in a hug of sugar dust,
Soft, yet firm, a taste we trust.
Oh, Swiss roll, your charm so grand,
You bring joy with every hand.

Semolina

In a kitchen, warm with evening's glow,
Semolina whispers soft and low,
In a pot, it dances, swirls, and spins,
A symphony of grains, where joy begins.

Milk and sugar join the tender song,
A creamy blend where flavours belong,
Golden grains, so humble and serene,
Transform into a dessert dream.

With a sprinkle of cinnamon, nutmeg's kiss,
Each spoonful is a moment of bliss,
Semolina pudding, a comfort so sweet,
A timeless treat, where memories meet.

Belgian Bun

A crown of icing, white and bright,
With a cherry on top, a delightful sight.

Soft and tender, a taste so fine,
A bite of heaven, simply divine.

With each morsel, joy is spun,
A simple pleasure, the Belgian bun.

A moment's escape, a sweet retreat,
In this pastry, life feels complete.

Banana Split

In a dish of porcelain, cold and white,
Nestles a trio of ice cream delight.
Scoops of vanilla, chocolate, and strawberry bright,
A symphony of flavours, a sweet, joyous sight.

Bananas sliced with care, golden and neat,
Cradling the scoops in their tender retreat.
Fudge drizzles down in a decadent stream,
Marshmallow clouds in a sugary dream.

Whipped cream peaks high like mountains of snow,
Adorned with cherries, their stems in a row.
Nuts sprinkled lightly, a crunchy embrace,
Each bite a journey, a smile on the face.

A banana split, a dessert so grand,
Crafted with love, by a gentle hand.
A taste of childhood, joy unconfined,
In every spoonful, sweet memories you'll find.

Fruit Trifle

In a crystal bowl, layers gleam so bright,
A symphony of colours, pure delight.
Custard smooth, a golden creamy stream,
Whipped cream clouds, soft as a dream.

Berries nestle in their juicy bed,
Ruby jewels, vibrant hues of red.
Sponge cake soaked in ambrosial wine,
Each bite a moment, truly divine.

Jelly shimmers with a playful wink,
A kaleidoscope of flavours in sync.
Oh, trifle, you're a feast for sight and taste,
A dessert where no single bite goes to waste.

Baked Alaska

Baked Alaska, a wonder, a culinary delight,
With layers of joy, it dazzles the sight.

Golden sponge cradles an ice cream dream,
Encased in meringue, as if spun from a beam.

A torch's kiss sets a caramel hue,
A dance between fire and frost to ensue.

Oh, Baked Alaska, a paradox divine,
You meld heat with chill, in perfect align.

In every bite, memories ignite,
Of warmth, of sweetness, of sheer delight.

Lemon Sorbet

Lemon sorbet, a citrus dream,
A cooling whisper, a sunlit beam.

Soft as silk on tongue it rests,
A burst of zest in every quest,

Sun-kissed lemons, tart and sweet,
In frozen form, they're such a treat.

A symphony of yellow hues,
Refreshing, crisp, a joy to muse,

Oh, lemon sorbet, pure delight,
You chase away the heat of night.

Raspberry Pavlova

Nestled in the hues of red and white,
Raspberry pavlova, a pure delight.

Crisp meringue, so tender and light,
Laced with whispers of a snowy night.

Creamy clouds that softly unfold,
Cradle berries, ruby and bold.

A dance of flavours, a lover's kiss,
In every bite, a moment of bliss.

Raspberry pavlova, art on a plate,
A timeless tale, where taste and beauty mate.

Snow Cone

In summer's blaze, beneath the golden sun,
A craving stirs that can't be left undone.
A symphony of colours, bright and bold,
In icy sweetness, childhood dreams unfold.

Crimson cherry, blue raspberry's hue,
A rainbow swirls in every frosty view.
The crunch of ice, the syrup's gentle flow,
A dance of flavours in the summer's glow.

Oh, snow cone bliss, a treat so pure and sweet,
You melt away the heat from head to feet.
With every bite, a memory is sown,
Of sunny days and joy — a snow cone.

Gelato

In a cup or on a cone so fine,
Gelato, sweet, a treat divine.

Your colours bright, your flavours bold,
A story of delight unfolds.

From pistachio green to lemon gold,
Strawberry red, a sight to behold.

Creamy texture, smooth and light,
Gelato brings such pure delight.

A frozen joy, a moment's plea,
In every scoop, pure ecstasy.

Apple Strudel

A pastry crafted with tender care,
Apple strudel, beyond compare.

Flaky crust, so light and crisp,
Encasing wonders, a sweetened wisp,

Of apples sliced, and spices bold,
A story of warmth, therein told.

Cinnamon whispers in every bite,
A dance of flavours, pure delight,

Raisin's plump, and nuts that cheer,
In apple strudel, joy draws near.

With each mouthful, the senses sing,
Of cozy hearths and winter's wing,

A symphony of sugar and spice,
In apple strudel, paradise.

Apple Charlotte

An apple charlotte takes its form,
A dessert that feels like home and warm.

Golden apples, crisp and sweet,
Nestled in a breaded seat,

Cinnamon whispers through the air,
A fragrant promise of love and care.

Baked to perfection, browned with grace,
It brings a smile to every face,

A timeless treat, both old and new,
Apple charlotte, a dream come true.

Apple Turnover

Golden crescents, crisp and warm,
A fragrant dance in pastry form,
With tender folds that gently break,
Unveiling treasures bakers make.

Inside, a symphony of spice,
Cinnamon whispers, sugar thrice,
Soft apples kissed by autumn's hand,
A taste of magic, simply grand.

In each bite, a comfort found,
A sweet embrace, joy unbound,
Apple turnovers, pure delight,
A pastry dream both day and night.

Lemon Drizzle Cake

Lemon drizzle, sweet and tart,
Crafted with a baker's heart.

Golden crumb with zesty hue,
Glazed in syrup, fresh and new,
Sugar crystals' sparkling dance,
Promises of joy, perchance.

Slice it thin or thick, your choice,
Each bite sings in citrus voice,
A simple cake, yet so divine,
With every taste, the stars align.

Fruit Salad

In a bowl, a rainbow bright,
A medley fresh, a pure delight,
Juicy gems of nature's yield,
In a fruit salad, joy revealed.

Mango's golden, sweet embrace,
Kiwi's emerald, gentle grace,
Strawberries, rubies, tart and sweet,
Together in a dance, they will meet.

Pineapple's tang, a zesty zing,
Blueberries, with their subtle swing,
Bananas, smooth and creamy hue,
A symphony of flavours, real and true.

Each bite a burst of summer's cheer,
A taste of sunshine, crystal clear,
In every piece, a story told,
Of orchards ripe, and sunlight's gold.

So gather round, and take a taste,
Of nature's bounty, none to waste,
For in this bowl of colours bright,
Lies pure enchantment, pure delight.

Custard Sauce

In the kitchen's gentle light, a cauldron hums,
A blend of sweetness, where vanilla drums,
Golden ribbons, silky smooth and bright,
Custard sauce, a dream in every bite.

Egg yolks dance with sugar, rich and warm,
Milk swirls in, a tender, creamy storm,
A touch of nutmeg, whispers of delight,
Custard sauce, the star of every night.

Over puddings, cakes, it gently flows,
A liquid velvet, in yellow glows,
Memories in each spoonful, never lost,
Custard sauce, a treasure, worth the cost.

Tiramisu

In a chilled embrace of sweet delight,
Tiramisu, a symphony in the night.
Layers of love, coffee-soaked dreams,
A dance of flavours, silky gleams.

Mascarpone whispers with a tender kiss,
Cocoa dusted, pure bliss.
Ladyfingers dipped in espresso deep,
In this dessert, memories sleep.

Italian heart in every bite,
Tiramisu, your beauty in light.
A cold indulgence, timeless and true,
In every spoonful, I find anew.

Handmade Belgian Chocolates
==========================

In a quaint little shop on a cobblestone street,
Where history and sweetness in harmony meet,
Artisans craft with deft, loving hands,
Handmade Belgian chocolates, like treasures from far lands.

Each piece a story, each bite a delight,
With flavours that dance, from morning to night,
Dark, milk, and white, with fillings so grand,
Caramel, hazelnut, and fruits of the land.

Wrapped in gold foil, a gift to the soul,
These chocolates of Belgium, they make one whole.
A taste of tradition, a touch of pure art,
Handmade with passion, they warm the heart.

Strawberry Fool

We mix our cream, both rich and clear,

A dessert, we all love dear,

Fold in the berries, crushed with care,

A swirl of red within the white affair.

Oh, strawberry fool, a treat divine,

Your taste a dance of sweet design,

A summer's dream in every spoonful,

A timeless pleasure, ever beautiful.

Jam Tart

Jam tarts, like jewels in a golden crown,
Their sweet aroma in the air floats down.

Crusts of butter, flaky and light,
Hold treasures within, a vibrant sight.

Strawberry, raspberry, apricot too,
Each one a burst of flavour, true.

Children's laughter and memories start,
With every bite of a tender heart.

In the world of treats, they play their part,
Oh, the timeless charm of a jam tart.

Biscoff Cake

In a world where sweetness reigns supreme,
There lies a cake that haunts my dream,
Biscoff, with your golden hue,
A symphony of flavours, rich and true.

Layers soft as whispered love,
Cradled in the skies above,
Cinnamon whispers, caramel sighs,
A dance of spices, a lover's guise.

Each bite a journey, a tender embrace,
Warmth and comfort in every trace,
Oh, Biscoff Cake, you steal my heart,
A masterpiece, a culinary art.

Rice Pudding

In a bowl of porcelain white,
Nestles a treat of soft delight,
Rice pudding, humble, mild, and sweet,
A symphony of warmth, complete.

Grains of rice, tenderly kissed,
By milk's embrace, a creamy mist.
A sprinkle of sugar, just enough,
To make the taste buds hum and puff.

Cinnamon whispers through the air,
With nutmeg's dance, a fragrant flair.
A comfort dish, both old and new,
Rice pudding, love in every hue.

Victoria Sponge Pudding

A humble cake begins to rise,
Victoria Sponge, a sweet surprise.

Golden sponge with texture fine,
Sugar kissed in every line.

A whisper of vanilla's charm,
Held in hands both safe and warm.

Layers spread with bright red jam,
And cream so rich, a perfect plan.

Each bite tells a story old,
Of teatime tales and hearts of gold.

A royal treat that's stood the test,
Of time and taste, it's simply best.

Victoria Sponge, in splendour sweet,
A timeless joy for all to eat.

Chocolate Sponge Pudding

Chocolate sponge, so rich and sweet,
An indulgence rare, a blissful feat.

A spoonful melts with heavenly grace,
Bringing a smile to every face.

With every bite, a story told,
Of comfort, love, and joy untold.

A simple dish, yet magic spun,
In chocolate sponge, our hearts are won.

Syllabub

In a bowl of cream so sweet,
A dream of flavours softly meet,
Syllabub, a name so quaint,
A dessert of old, without restraint.

A whisper of lemon's zest,
In frothy peaks, it finds its nest,
Wine or sherry, just a dash,
Mixes in with gentle splash.

Elegance in every bite,
A taste of history, pure delight,
Syllabub, in evening's glow,
A timeless treat from long ago.

Eves Pudding

In an orchard bathed in golden light,
Where apples blush and trees stand tall,
A secret recipe takes flight,
Eve's pudding, the jewel of fall.

Beneath a crust of tender embrace,
Lies fruit that whispers autumn's song,
Sweet and tart in a loving chase,
A harmony where both belong.

Creamy custard crowns the delight,
Warmth that melts the heart and soul,
On chilly nights, a beacon bright,
Eve's pudding, making spirits whole.

Gather 'round with friends and kin,
As laughter mingles with the steam,
In every bite, a tale within,
Of simple joys and dreams that gleam.

So let us raise a spoon and cheer,
To this dessert of humble grace,
For Eve's pudding, year after year,
Brings comfort in its sweet embrace.

Welsh Cakes

In a kitchen warm with love and light,
The scent of Welsh cakes brings delight,
Golden rounds on griddles dance,
A culinary romance.

From flour fine and currents sweet,
To butter rich, a simple treat,
A heritage in every bite,
Shared 'neath the soft Welsh twilight.

With sugar dust and tender crumb,
They sing of hearths from which they come,
Tradition's taste, both old and new,
In every Welsh cake, hearts renew.

Treacle Tart

Golden sweetness, a slice of art,
In the kitchen, treacle tart.
Crust so crisp, and filling bright,
A confectioner's pure delight.

Molasses rich, a syrupy stream,
Swirled within a baker's dream.
Lemon zest, a tangy kiss,
Adds to this dessert's sweet bliss.

With each bite, nostalgia sings,
Of childhood joys and simple things.
Treacle tart, a timeless treat,
Where old and new flavours meet.

Lemon Tart

In a golden crust, a tale unfolds,
A lemon tart, where sunshine moulds.
Beneath its glaze, a treasure lies,
A burst of zest, where flavour flies.

The tangy kiss, so sweetly sings,
A dance of citrus on angelic wings.
Its tender heart, a silken dream,
Where sugar whispers, 'neath a creamy seam.

Upon the plate, it sits with grace,
A perfect treat, in every trace.
Oh, lemon tart, so bright, so true,
A slice of joy, in every hue.

Flapjacks

Golden disks of warmth and cheer,
Flapjacks on the griddle near,
Bubbling batter, rising high,
Lifting spirits to the sky.

Morning light, a gentle hue,
Syrup's kiss, a sweet adieu,
Butter melting, pools of gold,
Stories of the day unfold.

Simple joy in every bite,
Comfort wrapped in morning light,
Flapjacks, friends, and laughter free,
A perfect start, for you and me.

Jam Roly Poly Pudding

A treat awaits on oven's edge,
A pudding wrapped in sweetened pledge.

Jam Roly Poly, soft and gold,
A story of sweet love retold.

With suet dough, so tender made,
And jam within, a secret laid.

As steam arises, hearts do warm,
In every slice, there's comfort's charm.

A taste of times both old and new,
In every bite, a love so true.

Sticky Toffee Pudding

In a cozy nook where warmth resides,
A golden dream of sweet delights,
Sticky toffee pudding, rich and grand,
A treasure born from baker's hand.

Molasses swirls in dark embrace,
With dates that lend a tender grace,
A sponge so moist, it melts away,
In caramel's dance, it loves to play.

Whipped cream or ice cream, cool and light,
Adorning plates in evening's light,
Each bite a symphony, pure and clear,
Sticky toffee pudding, bring us cheer.

Summer Pudding

In summer's glow, where berries burst,
A treat is born, to quench our thirst.
With crimson hues and flavours grand,
Sweet summer pudding takes its stand.

Beneath the sun, in gardens wide,
Raspberries, strawberries, side by side,
Blackcurrants and blueberries blend,
In harmony, their juices send.

Soft bread embraces, as they meld,
A symphony of tastes, upheld.
Chilled delight, on plates displayed,
A summer dream, in layers laid.

Each spoonful brings the season near,
A bite of sunshine, pure and clear.
In summer's warmth, a memory free,
Of pudding shared, 'neath the old oak tree.

Apple and Blackcurrant Pie

Golden crust, so crisp and light,
Holds treasures sweet, a pure delight.

Apples, tart, and juicy, blend,
With blackcurrants, their flavour's friend.

Tumbled together in a sugared embrace,
A symphony of taste, a dance of grace.

Slice by slice, the pie reveals,
A medley rich that gently heals.

With every bite, a story unfolds,
Of autumn's bounty, pure and bold.

Iced Doughnut

In a bakery's warm embrace, sweet delight,
An iced doughnut sits under sugary light.
With a glaze that sparkles like morning dew,
It calls to the heart, a treat to pursue.

Round and golden with a halo of frost,
A simple pleasure, no thoughts of the cost.
Sprinkles like stars on a canvas so sweet,
A bite of this treasure, the moment's complete.

Soft and tender, a hug for the soul,
A doughnut iced perfectly, making us whole.
In every layer, a story is spun,
Of joy, of warmth, and of simple fun.

Lemon Meringue Pie

Golden crust, so crisp and light,
Baked to perfection, a true delight.

Zesty lemon curd, both tart and sweet,
A symphony of flavours, a citrus treat.

Bright as the morning, fresh as the dew,
A taste of summer in every chew.

Whipped meringue, like clouds on high,
Peaks of snow against a sapphire sky.

Soft and airy, sweet with grace,
A final touch to this dessert's embrace.

A slice of joy, a piece of cheer,
A lemon meringue pie, always near.

Blackout Cake

Layers of darkness, a cocoa dream,
Whispering secrets in a chocolate stream.

Velvet shadows, dense and profound,
With each bite, a symphony of flavours resound.

Frosting like silk, a decadent sweep,
A dance of delight, in every piece we keep.

Blackout Cake, a nocturnal delight,
Crafted with passion in the heart of the night.

Indulgence so pure, it's more than just taste,
A moment of bliss, never in haste.

Lemon Cheesecake

Golden crust, a buttery embrace,
Holds a creamy dream in place.

Zest of lemon, bright and bold,
Swirls of sunshine, tales untold.

Tangy whispers, sweet delight,
Dance upon the tongue, ignite.

Each bite a symphony, soft and clear,
Echoes of joy, memories near.

A slice of heaven, pure and sweet,
In lemon cheesecake, life's complete.

Boston Cream Pie

Sitting pretty in the bakers shop window,
Fresh Boston cream pies all in a row.

Golden sponge with a custard heart,
A decadent blend of culinary art.

Beneath the glaze of chocolate sheen,
Lies a story sweet and keen.

Whisked with care, love's tender touch,
In each bite, memories clutch.

From Boston's streets to far and wide,
This humble pie holds boundless pride.

A taste of comfort, rich and true,
A timeless treat, forever new.

Carrot Cake

With spices rich and flavours deep,
A carrot cake, a joy to keep.

Golden carrots, grated fine,
Mix with flour, oh so divine.

Cinnamon whispers, nutmeg sings,
A symphony of simple things.

Cream cheese frosting, smooth and white,
Covers layers, pure delight.

Each bite a journey, sweet and grand,
A taste of comfort, home's own hand.

In every crumb, a story lies,
Of warmth and love and sweet goodbyes.

A carrot cake, both rich and light,
A timeless treat, a sweet delight.

Fondant Fancies

In a bakery bright, where the sweet dreams reside,
Lies a confection, a joy to the eyes,
Fondant fancies, so dainty and neat,
With pastel hues, a sugary treat.

Each little cake, a square of delight,
Wrapped in fondant, so soft and so light,
A sponge so tender, with layers to savour,
Filled with buttercream, a rich, creamy flavour.

A drizzle of icing, a cherry on top,
In a world full of sweets, these never will flop,
So here's to fondant fancies, so lovely and grand,
A bite-sized piece of enchantment, from a baker's skilled hand.

Empire Biscuit

Beneath the tartan skies so fair,
A treat awaits with tender care,
Scottish Empire Biscuits bright,
A sweet delight, a pure delight.

Two tender cookies, crisp and round,
With jammy goodness tightly bound,
A kiss of sugar on the top,
Where cherries bright invite a stop.

In Highland homes and city's hum,
They bring a taste of Scotland's charm,
A bite of history, pure and sweet,
Where past and present softly meet.

So raise a biscuit, toast the day,
In Scotland's heart, they've found their way,
A simple joy, a moment's bliss,
In every Empire Biscuit kiss.

Mud Cake

Butter melts like golden dreams,
Sugars fold in gentle streams.
Eggs are cracked with tender care,
Whisked into a creamy affair.

Flour joins the luscious blend,
Creating textures that will transcend.
Baked to perfection, a decadent embrace,
Mud cake, a heavenly grace.

Dense and moist with flavour deep,
A slice of bliss for all to keep.
A treat to share, a joy to make,
A timeless love, of mud cake.

Chocolate Yule Log

In winter's embrace, where the frost nips the air,
A festive delight awaits with tender care,
A Chocolate Yule Log, rich and divine,
Its presence a symbol of joy, pure and fine.

Rolled to perfection with a soft, spongy cake,
Swirled with cream filling, a dream to partake,
Dressed in ganache, dark and smooth,
Hints of sweet memories in every groove.

Adorned with holly, dusted in snow,
A slice of warmth as the cold winds blow,
In candlelight's glow, where laughter's bright,
The Chocolate Yule Log makes the season right.

Birthday Cake

A symphony of sugar, butter, and cream,
A canvas of frosting where candles gleam,
Layers of joy, stacked high with delight,
A birthday cake, the star of the night.

Whispers of vanilla, chocolate, or spice,
Each slice a portal to memories nice,
Celebrations past and dreams anew,
In every bite, a wish comes true.

Candles flicker, wishes take flight,
Surrounded by love, hearts feel light,
A sweet serenade in every crumb and flake,
Oh, the magic of a birthday cake.

Plum Pudding

In the heart of winter, when snowflakes gleam,
There's a warmth in kitchens, a cook's sweet dream.
A dessert so rich, in spices dressed,
Steamed plum pudding, the season's best.

Cinnamon whispers and nutmeg's embrace,
Raisins and currants find their place.
Molasses deep and suet so fine,
All meld together, a taste divine.

Steamed gently for hours, in cloth wrapped tight,
Emerges a treasure, a pure delight.
With brandy butter or cream to pour,
Steamed plum pudding, forever adored.

Banana Fritters

In the heart of golden twilight, a sizzle sings,
A melody of warmth in the fryer's embrace,
Banana fritters, a taste of simple things,
Crisp and tender, a culinary grace.

Batter whispers secrets as it wraps the fruit,
Transforming humble slices into treasures rare,
Golden-brown crescents, a sweet pursuit,
In the kitchen's glow, they dance in the air.

Sugar dusts like fairy tales, a sprinkle light,
Sweetening the crisp with a touch of delight,
Each bite a journey, a moment so bright,
Deep fried banana fritters, dreams take flight.

Chelsea Bun

In a cozy bakery where dreams are spun,
Lies the magic of a Chelsea bun.
Golden dough rolled with love and care,
Cinnamon whispers fill the air.

Raisins nestled in a sweet embrace,
Brown sugar dances, leaving a trace.
A swirl of warmth in each tender bite,
Morning's delight, an afternoon's light.

Glazed with sweetness, a final kiss,
Oh, Chelsea bun, pure bliss.
From oven's heart to eager hands,
You carry joy across the lands.

Eccles Cakes

Golden pastry, crisp and light,
Encasing treasures, hidden from sight,
Eccles cakes, a baker's delight,
A bite of history, pure and bright.

Currants nestled, sweet and dark,
Spiced with secrets, a fragrant spark,
Sugared top, a glistening mark,
Of Lancashire's love, a timeless arc.

From oven's warmth, they grace the plate,
A treat for all, we celebrate,
With every mouthful, memories sate,
Eccles cakes, a taste of fate.

Currant Teacakes

In a cottage kitchen, warm and bright,
Where sunbeams dance with morning light,
The scent of currants fills the air,
Teacakes baking with tender care.

Golden crusts and sweet delight,
Soft and tender, a baker's might,
Currants dot the fluffy dough,
Gems of flavour, a subtle glow.

With each bite, a story told,
Of hearths and homes in days of old,
A simple pleasure, pure and sweet,
Currant teacakes, a timeless treat.

White Chocolate and Peach Trifle

White chocolate whispers, smooth and sweet,
Meets peachy dreams where summer heat.

Layers of joy, so tenderly laid,
Creamy and rich, a sweet serenade.

Peaches so golden, kissed by the sun,
Twirl with the chocolate, two become one.

A trifle so lovely, a symphony in taste,
Moments of bliss that cannot be replaced.

Each spoonful a story, a memory unfurled,
White chocolate and peach, a treasure of the world.

Ginger Cake

In a warm kitchen, what a sight,
A ginger cake takes shape tonight.
Spices mingle, rich and bold,
In a batter spun like threads of gold.

Molasses drips, a sweet embrace,
In the air, an aromatic grace.
Ginger whispers tales untold,
Of hearths and homes in days of old.

Toasty brown, it cools with care,
A confection made with love to share.
Each soft bite a spicy cheer,
A timeless treat that draws us near.

Fruit Loaf

Golden crust with hints of spice,
Each tender slice, a taste so nice.

Raisins, currants, gems of old,
Nestled deep in doughy folds.

Candied peel, a citrus spark,
A symphony within the dark.

Butter spreads and melts away,
A morning treat to start the day.

Fruit loaf, comfort, simple and grand,
A loving touch from baker's hand.

Chocolate Mousse

In a dish of velvet, smooth and deep,
Lies a dream, a whisper, a secret to keep.
Chocolate mousse, a delight so sweet,
A symphony of flavours, where passions meet.

Rich cocoa drifts in airy light,
A dance of shadows in the night.
Silken texture, a lover's kiss,
Pure indulgence, a moment of bliss.

Spoons dive gently, worlds collide,
In each bite, joy does reside.
Chocolate mousse, a heaven found,
In its embrace, hearts are bound.

Rocky Road

In a kitchen warm with light's gentle embrace,
A symphony begins, a sweet, delightful race.
Flour and sugar, a dance in the air,
Cocoa powder joins, a chocolaty affair.

Marshmallows soft, like clouds in the sky,
They tumble and twirl, like a dream passing by.
Nuts crackle and pop, a crunchy delight,
In this rocky road, they join the sweet flight.

Baked to perfection, biscuits golden and warm,
A treat to remember, a comforting norm.
Each bite a journey, through textures and taste,
A culinary wonder, not a crumb to waste.

Crème Brûlée

In a world of sweet, where dreams delight,
There lies a dish, in golden light.
A silky whisper, soft and pure,
Crème brûlée, a love so sure.

Beneath the surface, crisp and fine,
A caramel kiss in perfect line.
A tap, a crack, reveals below,
The creamy depths in gentle glow.

Vanilla whispers, rich and sweet,
A dance of flavour, pure and neat.
A symphony in every bite,
Crème brûlée, a sweetened night.

Yoghurt and Buttermilk Panna Cotta

In the dawn of flavours, a tale is spun,
Of yogurt and buttermilk, kissed by the sun.
They dance in a panna cotta's creamy embrace,
A symphony of textures, a delicate grace.

Yogurt, with tang, brings a whisper of zest,
A hint of the morning, with vigour and jest.
Buttermilk follows, with a soft, milky glide,
A velvety partner, in whom dreams confide.

Together they merge, in a silken delight,
In each tender bite, a taste of pure light.
A dessert that sings of both tart and sweet,
Where dairy and daydreams so seamlessly meet.